Come on in...

*we've been dying
to meet you...*

CW00890882

GHOSTS!

Creepy tales from Chislehurst Caves

Acknowledgements

Thanks to James Geary Gardner for allowing me and my schoolboy friends to work (and play!) in the Caves in 1950's; to his son Jimmy Gardner who now owns the Caves; Terry Hunt, the Caves Manager; Cave Guides Paul Andrews, Jason Desporte, Jeffry Hooton, Rod LeGear, Dan McLean, Chris Manning-Perry, Chrissy Selby, Desmond Tyler, Barbara Viahakis, Nick Winter, Stefan Zambinski and many visitors on tours who have added to my knowledge of the history and folklore of the Caves, my friends in the Bromley Local History Society, also to the helpful staff in the Local History departments of the Bromley and Orpington Libraries, the Orpington Museum, and many second-hand bookshops, especially Badger Books of Worthing, for aiding and abetting me in my researches. To my wife Jenny for years of encouragement, and daughter Catherine for hours of proofreading. And especially to www.pcrepairscroydon.com for saving me from a nasty virus which tried to eat this book up! Not forgetting, of course, the various spooks and other entities of the Caves – couldn't have written this without you! Thanks to them: all errors and omissions are mine alone.

All illustrations are from the Author's collection, except for: Pages 9, 16, 48 Caves Archives; map on page 4 painted on a wall in the Hospital by the Red Cross staff during the War, with later damage repaired by Terry Hunt; 28, 47, Paul Andrews; page 53 Debbie Fairweather. Victorian pictures pages 56, 57, 58 from "Ghosts – The Illustrated History" by Peter Haining, published by Sidgwick & Jackson in 1974. Cover picture is a detail from the carving in the Caves produced by Sandy Brown.

Produced using Microsoft Word; Serif *Photoplus* and *Pageplus*.
Edited by Brian Williamson, nullpublishing.co.uk

Contents

Memorise this map before you enter. It will improve your chances of coming out again!

4

Ghosts ... and things that go bump in the dark.

Mankind has always had a fear of the dark. Huddling together round the camp fire must have been one of the earliest social gatherings, and at night, most outdoor movement stopped. Apart from creatures of the night to be wary of, there were also our own ancestors. After all, people were so superior to the animals, that it seemed unbelievable that we could completely die, for although bodies might cease to work and be burned or put away, surely some trace would remain? So all over the world, as well as towns for the living, there were towns for the dead. So, as well as all the day-to-day affairs to worry about, you had to satisfy the demands of the dead, too. Not only to keep them happy, but to stop them coming back uninvited. When the belief in evil spirits causing disease gradually became overcome by more modern thinking, there were still some things that couldn't be explained away. Such things that might remain usually seemed to stay in the dark. Chislehurst Caves are very dark, so visitors still tend to be aware of the possibility of "something" being there in the darkness. Although Chislehurst Caves are really a mine, chalk is unusual in that it is strong enough to support a roof without the need for pit-props. The occasional brick or concrete arch or column is usually there because a house has been built on the land above. Curtain walls dotted around are mainly wartime relics, built either to create rooms for offices or toilets, etc, to direct airflow from the ventilation fans or, more recently, to separate off parts used by *Labrynthe,* a private "dungeons'n'dragons" live role playing club. This club uses a separate entrance, just by the car park next to the cafe, which has its own story. The wartime owner wrote just after the Second World War :

> The Caves were first leased to the present owner around 1920, with the notion of starting a Mushroom farm underground, the conditions being ideal. However, for various reasons the whole project was dropped. The owner being a keen speleologist started to explore and excavate. A great deal of the supernatural now seems to play a part in the explorations. At

5

this time there was no entry on the level ground. The only entrance being on land owned by the "Bickley Arms Hotel", a Trust House. An elderly couple in the 1890's remembered when they were children getting into the Caves through a fox hole, adjacent to the present entrance at the "Bickley Arms". It had not been possible to discover another exit or entrance, and after several fruitless months hopes were rather low. The owner's Mother had a friend, a very charming Scottish lady, who had psychic powers, and it was suggested that she might like to help. One day she arrived, and after taking a lamp and leading the way through the labyrinth of Caves from one blocked chamber to another, finally came to a very small corridor blocked with sand. Here, she announced, the digging should commence, and an entrance would be found. She further predicted that one day, at lunch time, a breakthrough would be made, and proceeded to describe the series of Caves that lay beyond.

Six months later, after digging through 200ft of sand, the owner was working on a large chalk face, stepped back quickly as the whole of the boulder fell outwards, not forwards as he expected, leaving a gaping hole. At the same time as this happened, colleagues called out to him that "lunch was ready". After lunch, all three went through the hole he had made, and the Caves beyond were just as the medium had described. This same lady also said, when standing on some rough ground outside the entrance, that she foresaw a vision of thousands of people camping out. This prediction was borne out in the Second World War, when the shelterers were camping out during the Air Raids in large numbers.

(Extract from a booklet published by the Caves' owner in the 1950's.)

During the Second World War, thousands of people lived and slept in the Caves. What did they feel about the experience? I have heard from a number of people who were there, and nobody seems to have been frightened of the place. Jill Cheeseman, in her book *A Child's Wartime Memories* about her experiences growing up as a shelterer in the Caves, tells stories of playing with other children in the Druids, while they were unoccupied. Not only does nobody claim to have been frightened, they all mention the happy, friendly atmosphere generated by the regular visitors. So if there is a "spirit of the Caves", it is more likely to be the remainder of the feeling of relief at reaching a place of safety, and the laughter of happy children. Although there are a few exceptions...

The Death Trap at the Cavaliers Entrance

This entrance is said to date back to the English Civil War, 1640-1660. The Caves were known to some of the locals, and it is said that a prominent Cavalier, a supporter of the King, Charles I, lived in a house on Old Hill, which lies over the Caves. The Chislehurst area generally supported Parliament and Oliver Cromwell, who, due to the shape of the helmets his soldiers wore, were known as Roundheads. It

was therefore prudent for local supporters of the King to keep their opinions to themselves and to make plans to leave hurriedly should the need arise - mobs tended to kill you first and ask questions afterwards in those days. His cunning plan was to dig a passageway down into the Caves. This started in his garden, or the woodland just behind and is unique in being the only entrance to the Caves which slopes - all the others are either flat (well, flattish, anyway) or vertical shafts. It is also a curving passageway, being about three-quarters of

7

a circle. Part way down, there is a vertical shaft dropping down into one of the cave passageways. The story is that he used to cover the top of this shaft with twigs and leaves, and scatter leaves on the floor. If he was pursued by the local Roundheads they might well charge down the passage letting their eagerness override their natural caution. There wouldn't be much light from a lantern or two, and if they didn't know what to expect, some of the mob could easily find themselves falling down the shaft. They would then be able to confirm or deny the story that the Cavalier had placed spikes at the bottom of the shaft. He would be waiting nearby, and if he heard the screams and the squelch when the unwanted visitors reached the bottom, he could either retire further into the Caves or perhaps leave by another exit.

The **grey figure** occasionally seen near here is reputed to be either a Roundhead caught in the trap or a Cavalier who forgot where he left the hole. The shaft continued to claim victims. In 1972 it was unblocked and used as the location for the escape shaft from the Tallium mines of Thalos in an episode of Dr Who (*The Mutants*) which was filmed in the Caves. One of the Guides took a party of friends to inspect the top of the shaft, and fell down, breaking both legs. Luckily for him, there were no spikes there then. After this, the shaft was firmly blocked up again! It is occasionally shown to special Birthday Party tours.

The Ghostly Druid

The most evocative picture of ghostly goings-on in the Caves is the picture taken of the Druids altar, apparently showing a translucent figure. The story behind this picture is that many years ago, before the First World War , in the days of black and white photographs using flash-powder for lighting, and before computers and modern photo-editing programs, an intrepid photographer set up his equipment and took several pictures in the Druids. When he developed his pictures later, the picture of the Druid Altar was seen to contain a figure he hadn't seen at the time. The resulting postcard has been popular with visitors ever since.

The Druid Altar

There are various stories connected with the Druid altar. Dr Nichols, a vice-President of the British Archaeological Society in 1903, described this part of the Caves as being Celtic, used as a Druid Temple. Most obvious is the altar itself. About hip height, convenient for using as a table, and with a small recess on the right hand side. Next to it is the "Priest's Alcove". What highlights this alcove from all other short dead-ends the tour passes is the quality of its workmanship. It has obviously been carefully chipped out, using hundreds of pick strokes, to an impressively accurate semi-circle. The roof has been shaped, too, into a not-so-impressive hemisphere. Whatever the reasons for it, somebody spent a lot of time and effort on this alcove. The workmanship of the "Altar" itself is less finished and quite rough in comparison. The wall behind it is partly shaped, but the top of the altar is quite rough. Perhaps it was once better finished and has subsequently been damaged - the Romans went around destroying all the Druid things they could find, so let's blame them, shall we?

According to Dr Nichols' imagination, what happened here was this. The passageway leading up to the altar leads from the maze of Caves and then curves to the left, facing up a long straight passageway to the altar itself. Imagine, if you will, a collection of people coming round the corner and moving slowly up to the altar. The group would include priests and prominent local people to act as witnesses, all led by a single figure, which tradition suggests was dressed in a white gown, and carrying a bowl or chalice, probably of carved wood, though perhaps of beaten bronze. We know that the Romans hated the Druids partly because of their indulgence in human sacrifice, though records also suggest that these were generally volunteers, deliberately allowing themselves to be killed in order to act as messengers to plead their tribe's case to the gods.

So we can imagine the sacrifice walking proudly at the head of the procession, though probably in a drunken or drug-induced state, not because the priests wanted them to depart happily, but more practically because they didn't want them to change their minds at the last minute. Whatever the victim was looking forward to, the rest of the procession was probably looking forward to the feast afterwards. No doubt there were sounds, as well - chanting, beating of drums and trumpets, or perhaps flutes. There could have been smells, too. The Romans used a brazier of burning pine cones at times like this, so there's no reason why the Druids shouldn't have thought of something similar, mingling with the scents of the burning torches of pine branches or perhaps apple wood.

As the victim reached the Altar, the Chief Priest would have come out of the alcove and addressed the procession. (Like Company Chairman or politicians today, I'm sure that if you gave a Druid priest an audience, he'd give a speech or a sermon). The victim would then place the bowl they had been carrying into the recess, and be helped onto the altar, laying feet higher than his or her head, with their head conveniently just above the bowl.

No doubt the Priest would continue to chant and perform his ceremonies to invoke the Gods (after all, he has only got one chance to get his big moment right). Then, when all the signs and portents were right (or the sacrifice was showing signs of changing their minds) the priest would step forward and cut the victim's throat. I expect there would be shouts and applause at this moment, both to celebrate the climax of the event, and to cover the sacrifice's last request to postpone the ceremony because she had just remembered she needed to return her library book. The collected blood in the bowl would, tradition says, be offered to the Gods.

In reality, this is all very unlikely to have happened in the Caves. Druids were a nature-spirit worshipping religion, and usually used open glades in woodland for their ceremonies, especially around large oak trees with mistletoe on them. This must be sacred, since it grew between earth and sky without needing roots. But however much you know it was unlikely to have happened here, in the half light and echoes about the altar it somehow becomes more possible.

You should try standing there in total darkness and complete silence, letting your imagination have free rein!

Tales from the Mushroom Growers

There have been no reported sightings of ghosts of sacrificial victims, but the Mushroom Growers working in the Druids in the 1930's handed down several stories.

Let Me OUT!

A story that seems to have been handed down over the years from the days when the mine was in regular use concerns an old-time chalk miner. He was cutting out chalk to burn for lime from a remote work face when the roof of the tunnel collapsed behind him. His colleagues dug frantically through the rubble to try to reach him but were beaten back by more falls. They attempted to get to him from another direction by tunnelling through the solid chalk but only encountered more falls. After a few days, attempts to retrieve his body were abandoned.

In the Second World War, when the Caves became one of the largest underground shelters in the country, a number of ventilation tunnels were dug in order to ensure that there was a good flow of fresh air throughout the caves. One of these small headings passed through the area of the ancient accident. This seems to have disturbed the spirit of the unfortunate miner. On a number of occasions since then it has been reported that the sound of what appears to be knocking and digging can be heard in this area coming from behind a pile of rock and sand. Fortunately, this area of the Caves is a long way from the 'tourist' routes!

Roman Soldier

A Roman Soldier in full uniform has been seen on several occasions, including during the War when he was seen by some children exploring a roped-off area of the Caves. He is supposed to have been murdered outside the Caves near the river. Why his spirit walks the Caves is not known.

The wartime sighting was noted in a letter as follows: *"It was always safe to allow children to play in the Caves, there were* no worries of anyone hurting them in those days, in fact we would watch out for each others children. One evening my little boy wanted to have a look around; I said "Now don't wander away from the people or you could get lost".

He took his young sister Dorothy and a friend. Some time later they all came running back, Dorothy with only one shoe. When I eventually calmed them down, Georgie, my little boy told me they had been chased by a Roman soldier. He even gave me a description of his dress. I told him not to be so stupid and to go back for Dorrie's shoe, but he was too terrified to go. Sadly, Georgie died at the age of thirty-four, and several years after, a member of the family brought a magazine back from the Caves for me. On the front page was a small picture of a Roman soldier who was said to be one of the many ghosts who haunt the Caves. I always ask myself, was Georgie privileged to see him?"

The Wonderful Cave Dog

Not all the apparitions are of humans. A dog has been heard barking, and has been seen by several people. An Edwardian guide used to bring his dog on the tours. He was known as "The Wonderful Cave Dog" as he was very good at finding lost tourists and leading them to safety. Maybe his ghost is still looking for lost souls to rescue! This postcard was sold at the Caves in 1910.

The Hunchback

A small figure described as a hunchback has been seem on a number of occasions. A well known artist, Frederick Herrick, visited the Caves in 1931. He usually painted advertising posters for the travel industry, featuring ships or railways, but he seems to have become interested in the Caves. His picture appears to be set in the Maze part of what looks like the Druids, with one of the lesser-known altars, and shows a small cloven-hoofed creature scampering around with two old Druid-like figures hiding away from him. Makes you wonder what happened next, doesn't it? The *Most Haunted* team reported a small creature they which they also described as a hunchback during their investigations in 2008.

Druid Princess

A misty figure thought to have been the ghost of a Druid Princess drowned in an underground stream was apparently often seen near the entrance to the Druids. She must have been disturbed by the arrival of thousands of shelterers during World War Two, for she has not been reported since.

The Haunted Pool

The atmosphere surrounding the area known as the Haunted Pool is damp and depressing. Obviously, it's dark - the only light is whatever you brought with you. If you stand there quietly, then you may start to hear sounds... This area of the Caves is apparently under a collection point for water – a kind of underground lake. The area of the Haunted Pool is close to an area where part of the roof fell in about 1860, apparently due to a build up of water behind a retaining wall round a stable above. The wall acted as a dam, and trapped such a weight of water that a section of cave roof collapsed.

Adults often complain of feeling a chill here, which is odd because there are several places near fan shafts that actually are colder at times, and they don't usually mention those. I have noticed several times that babies tend to get disturbed as they come to the pool. Any babies with a tour are usually woken up when the echo is demonstrated by the Druid Altar, but have settled down again by the time they reach the Haunted Pool about five minutes later. Here they often start crying again, apparently for no particular reason. The wail of a baby, and its attendant echoes, certainly add to the atmosphere! Strangely, most babies settle down again as soon as the tour moves on.

The Murder at the Pool

The story of the murder at the pool has proved to be difficult to verify. There are several versions, but the common elements are that a man, by some accounts a flint knapper, which would put the date as somewhere in the 1700's, visited this area with a woman, apparently his wife. He is reported to have knocked her out with a lump of rock, weighted her body down with lumps of chalk and thrown her into the pool, either to drown her or just to hide the body.

But although the event took place underground, in the darkness in a remote part of the Caves the crime was discovered about two weeks later by another man evaluating the area for growing mushrooms. He was checking out the pool for use to water his proposed crop when he looked down through the crystal clear water and saw the body. Unfortunately, the event predates the earliest local newspapers, and although today's local newspaper *News Shopper* even goes as far as naming the lady as Mary Jane Beckett, I have been unable to locate any contemporary reports of her death or any subsequent trial. The water in the Haunted Pool has since the Second World War been about two feet deep, and in 2011 was down to about a foot, possibly due to global warming, but earlier records suggest that it used to be much deeper. It is probable that the pond was filled up with rubble dug out from the new link tunnel to prevent sheltering children from drowning. Additional rubble can be seen heaped by the entrance to the tunnel, and piled up in two of the side passages nearby.

The White Lady

The pool area is supposed to be haunted by the lady murdered there. Her restless spirit is supposed to roam around the area, and she has been reported sitting on the rocks at the back of the pool, crying quietly. One guide reported seeing a mist collecting on top of the pool, collecting together into a human shape, but he didn't hang around to see what happened next... The area of the Caves surrounding the Haunted Pool was even more isolated before the Second World War. Visitors today usually approach the Haunted Pool from the Druid Altar and the demonstration of the echo, passing through the little link tunnel known as Snowy Way. However, this was not excavated until the Caves were filling up with shelterers in 1941, when it was dug to allow access between the Roman and Druid sections and improve air

17

circulation from the newly installed fans. So this was then a dead end in more ways than one...   There is certainly a change of atmosphere when you come through the little link tunnel, which I try to explain away to myself as being due to the damper atmosphere round the pool.

The ceiling of the cave hereabouts used to be sprinkled with drops of water in two distinct areas. They fell at random, some into the pool, and some onto a heap of chalky debris nearly filling a short side passage. Water dripping into water produced a range of splashes, but the water on chalk can have strange effects. Regular drips tend to bore out a tiny hole, and following drips will then fall in the same place, forcing out the air from the hole. Since all the tiny holes will be different sizes and depths, a variety of sounds are produced. Mix this with the echoes, and you get an eerie atmosphere. However, all this has been altered by climate change. All the damp places and drips in the Caves are now much reduced - but not gone completely, so it's still not a good idea to look up with your mouth open!

The Challenge
Because of the eerie atmosphere and the story of the murder, a challenge grew up in the late 1950's to spend the night alone by the pool. The rules were established as one person with six candles, and a sleeping-bag. The guide would leave, promising to return the following morning.   On most occasions, the challenger would change their mind as soon as the light from the guide's lamp started to disappear round the corner, and follow him out! A trail was laid so that challengers could find their way out if they needed to.   Several challengers found that they just couldn't stay where they had been put, and simply wondered away, too flustered to follow the trail. However, they soon found their way to the guide when he came back in the morning, either shouting to him, or attracted to his torch like moths to a flame. One of the

challengers decided to light all his candles at once. Naturally, they all started to go out at the same time, too. Suddenly realising his situation, he decided to run out as fast as possible by the light of his sole remaining candle. As anybody knows who has tried to run with a candle, this isn't a good idea, as it immediately goes out, and splashes hot wax on your hand as well. By this time he was past all reason, and just kept on running ... straight into a wall. He was found the following morning, still unconscious.

However, he didn't win any reward, as it was felt that being unconscious didn't count! The one successful challenger in the 35 years of the challenge, was a policeman, Tony Bayfield. He became convinced that he wasn't alone by the pool, and moved a little way down the cave. He stumbled over a piece of flint, and stood all night carving a picture of a horse on a nearby wall. Not a very good picture, it must be said, but if you were there, with the light of a single candle, and convinced that "something" was standing just behind you, looking over your shoulder and breathing down your neck, it is unlikely that you could do any better!

The policeman couldn't explain why he picked on a horse to carve, but it is coincidental that the Haunted Pool was partly framed by a roof-fall around 1860, when some stables collapsed into the caves. Apparently the screams of terrified horses have occasionally been reported in that area. Could this have influenced his choice of subject?

The Guides' Experience

Two of the Caves Guides decided that this challenge was too good to miss, and they decided to join in themselves. After all, Guides often travel round the Caves alone, so sleeping down there should be no problem. Dave Duker and Chris Perry were well able to take care of themselves, but in order to undertake the trial they had to follow the same rules as everyone else. This had always been a solo challenge, so they couldn't stay together. They got permission to carve a commemorative plaque, and put it just by the horse produced by the only successful challenger. On it, they noted a 12 hour vigil, which turned out to be a little optimistic. They produced the plaque together just before the attempt.

On the attempt night, when the last public tour had left, Dave and Chris went to the Haunted Cave and prepared to settle down. They couldn't stay together, so they tossed a coin to see who would move away. Chris won (or was it lost?) and moved away round a corner to kip down just by the plaque they had carved. He figured that staying by the horse carved by the only winner of the challenge would be a good idea. But things didn't go according to plan...

The support team saw them settled down, with their flasks of coffee and supply of candles. Both men got into their sleeping bags, and tried to get to sleep. To ensure fair play, a tape recorder was set up in between them to record if they communicated with each other. (Alright, you were thinking of video cameras and other gizmos. But this was 1985, and a tape recorder *was* hi-tech in those days!)

The original tape is kept locked away for safe keeping, but I managed to borrow it briefly for review. The biggest stumbling block is that there are no timing details on the tape. We are all used today to police interviews on television programmes where the officer at the interview – be they Frost, Morse or an American detective – will always talk to the tape recorder at the start of the interview to note the time and who is present. This wasn't done, so sometimes it's difficult to be sure who is talking – or screaming!

Listening to the tape there's obviously a lot of hiss and crackling as the two settled down. Remember that the tape recorder was on the floor between the two, and about ten meters from them. Add in sundry noises from dripping water, all confused by echoes, and even the first hand evidence from the tape is sometimes difficult to interpret. This is what I have been able to make out. Woken up suddenly in the middle of the night and faced with a crisis does occasionally lead to the use of language of which mother wouldn't approve, and any such has been removed so as not to offend older readers - I doubt if the younger ones would mind!

There's lots of background hiss at the start of the tape, then suddenly, apparently at about two thirty in the morning, lots of noise, shouts and a scream, which woke Dave up.

Transcript from the original tape:
Shouts from Chris.

Shouts of *"Chris",* getting louder as Dave rushes towards the tape recorder then fading as he rushes to where Chris is lying.

You can hear Chris groaning in the background.

Dave talks quietly to Chris, then shouts his name.

"Chris! Chris mate! Chris! Are you all right?" Chris' noisy breathing can be heard on the tape.

"I think I better get help. Stay there."

21

A problem he hadn't anticipated was that they had locked themselves in – and Chris had the keys. The entrance to the Caves was out in the open then, and the Café and the support group were in a hut some 25 yards away. There were no houses nearby, and the immediate area was quite bleak and barren. They didn't want anybody finding the Caves entrance open and wandering in, especially one of their "friends" coming in to try to scare them, so they had closed and locked the door behind them.

The tape continues with sounds of footsteps passing the tape recorder, then returning. Probably Dave going back to where he had been sleeping, searching for the keys.

"Chris. Chris. Chris. Where's the keys, mate? I'll get some help. Where's the keys, mate? Don't worry, I'll get some help.

Stay there. I'll get some help." Dave finds the keys in Chris' pocket. *"You all right?"*

Getting no answer, Dave leaves to run to the surface. All quiet except for the occasional sound of Chris' groaning and heavy breathing. At one time there's some thumps and moans, as though Chris was rolling around.

Voices in the distance, coming closer. Footsteps, getting louder. Shouts of *"Chris!"*

Two people talking at the same time. *"Chris"* and *"Are you all right?"*

"We'll have to see about getting him out"

"You look in a bad state now, mate."

The rescuers crowd round Chris, and discuss what to do next. Chris occasionally shouts a word or two, raising echoes which makes it very difficult to make out what is being said. Chris is asked several times if he is OK, with only a groan for answer.

At least one more person had joined the group, and all are talking together. Only a few phrases can be made out:

"... pushed him over, in a position like that, and he moved again.   The situation's not good."

"Let's help him up to the top, get some air."

"We were doing quite well, then that happened."

"I'll get my torch".

The sound of voices diminish, as the party moves off taking Chris to the surface.   The recording ends abruptly, presumably when somebody remembers the tape recorder, turns it off and carries it away with them. Chris was unable to walk, so was carried out by his friends, and he remembered nothing of the journey or his ambulance trip to hospital until he woke the following morning. On arrival in casualty, Chris was checked from top to toe, and there seemed no obvious cause for his condition. The only problem seemed to be a bruise developing on his shoulder, so he was sent for an x-ray. This showed him to have a bad dislocation, the operation on which has left him with a six inch scar. The Doctors said that it looked as though someone (or something?) had pulled his arm violently upwards, as though trying to drag him away. The difficulty is that it couldn't possibly have happened that way. Chris had his arms tucked inside his sleeping bag when he was found... None of the participants saw or heard anything out of the ordinary, and the events of that night have never been explained. But the Caves Management decided that since somebody had been hurt, the challenge would be stopped.

The Challenge was stopped after that incident in 1985 and has not been allowed since, so please don't ask!

But perhaps they could have chosen a more suitable night than Halloween for their attempt? Chris Perry spent several days in hospital, and continued his job as a guide until March

2004. Dave Duker returned to his guiding job but left for good a few weeks later, when he won a small fortune on football pools. When they tossed that coin by the pool neither of them knew how much was riding on the outcome.

The two Guide Challengers were allowed to carve a plaque, which they did the day before their attempt, so they got the time wrong!

Ghost Hunting

There have been many Ghost Hunts over the years, most of which have left no trace. The "no overnight stays" rule was introduced in 1985. Since then, some events have taken place during special evening tours, where a group paid for a special private tour after the Caves have closed to the public. For their money, they get the services of their own guide, and could go anywhere that was safe to go. These tours are for parties of people who just want a longer tour than usual, but occasionally they used to bring along tables and chairs, set up their own equipment and hold a séance where ever they fancied. However, a few people abused this privilege, and it has now been stopped. Almost invariably the organisers of these events used to promise to let us know what they found, but they never did, which is why there are no such reports in this book.

Most Haunted

There has been one notable exception to the "no overnight stays" rule, however. One group, much more professional than all the others, persuaded the owner to make just one exception. This was the *Most Haunted* crew from Living TV, who had exceptional experience - and a very good insurance policy of their own, too. They visited the Caves in February 2008, and found enough material to produce two one-hour-long TV programmes, which were first broadcast on Sky in April 2008. Some of their findings were remarkably similar to tales I had already collected together for this book, which they had not seen before they came to the Caves. The Caves Guides were all pleasantly surprised that the "presences" found during this investigation generally tied in very well with our understanding, and with the occasional verifiable record. I rewrote some sections of the draft manuscript for this book, adding their comments to my original stories. However, requests for permission to use photographs taken during their visit and details of the people involved were never answered, so no pictures from them, either! However, two one-hour programmes were produced and broadcast, so a hunt through the Internet will probably lead you to them, if you wish to see them. They certainly raise a few questions!

A Phantom Horse?

The Guides are often approached by Mediums who claim to be able to "feel the vibrations" about the caves. We guides discuss these pronouncements amongst ourselves and we usually get a laugh out of the seriousness with which these stories are told. And you are right if you feel you detect a note of scepticism. If any of them told us something new which was checkable, that would be interesting, or if they all felt the same thing at the same place, that could give us pause for thought. But to be told that "there is a distinct presence here!" when everyone picks a different place, or "I sense the aura of a sad child around here" is without meaning - with thousands of years of use, and thousands of people sleeping down there during the War, there can't be many corners where there hasn't, at some time or another, been an unhappy child, although those who were there all stress the happy nature of the place when seen through the eyes of the children.

However, even my scepticism has been challenged. At one place on each tour I usually stop and ask my party if they missed anything or if there are any questions. On a tour in mid-2005 a lady asked me about horses in the caves, and I gave her the usual explanation about the scrapes on the walls in places suggesting wheeled vehicles, presumably used to take chalk out of the Caves during mining operations. I also explained that there was a horse, presumably a pit-pony, mentioned as being used during the War. "No", she said, "I felt the presence of a thoroughbred horse, not a working one. It was that that kicked the guide in his sleeping bag." It's the only explanation I have ever heard for the injury occurring *inside* his sleeping bag. And it did happen where the policemen carved his horse on the wall. Could there be a connection?

The Woman with the Pram

Since the War when up to 15,000 people used the Caves as an air raid shelter, a young woman has sometimes been seen pushing a pram through the Roman caves. She is never seen close up but all reports say she is smiling. It is thought that she was a shelterer from Walworth in South-East London who was persuaded by her sister to use the local shelter one night instead of travelling to the Caves which she had done for almost a year. That night the shelter near East Lane, Walworth took a direct hit and all inside were killed. It seemed that her spirit returned to where she felt safe.

Derek, the Whistling Ghost

Early in 2007, it was discovered that some of the walls put up in a rush in 1940 were beginning to show their age, and no longer came up to the standard required by the latest Building Regulations. Since the Caves are open to the public, Health & Safety regulations meant that we had to do something about them. Houses have been built on top of the Caves since the War, and what was good enough then, is not good enough now. In most cases this simply meant building another wall in front of the existing one, but sometimes it was considered better to close off an occasional dead-end and fill it with concrete grout. The bulk of the Caves were unaffected, but one tiny section which used to contain an office used by a one-time guide named Derek was closed off for ever. Derek had a habit of whistling between his teeth as he pottered round the Caves when he was working, and it was said that you could always hear him coming! Ever since builders started to measure up and prepare the room, people have reported hearing a faint whistling around that area at times. If it continues to be reported, we may have to build him another office! The *Most Haunted* team also reported hearing whistling around there.

Fatal Meditation

A story I and my schoolboy friends were told by James Gardner (the father of the current owner) in 1955 concerns a man who broke his way into the Caves and died there a few years after the War. I researched this in Bromley library, from contemporary newspaper reports, and this is his sad story.

After the Second World War the Caves were left empty and unoccupied. This was typical of the time: people had just endured years of war, and although the War had ended, there was still food rationing, and shortages of most everyday goods and bomb damage everywhere. There was no interest whatsoever in paying for a tour round an old air raid shelter, and the Caves were closed up and left. There were several possible ways in, and local schoolboys occasionally broke in and wandered around. One such boy, Patrick Mulhearn, went into the Caves with some friends one Sunday afternoon in late October, 1949, perhaps as a Halloween dare. They found more than they expected...

As reported at the time, they were exploring the Caves by the light of pocket torches. "My mate said 'Look over there', then he said 'it's a body' and we all turned and ran out". He did not report his discovery until he got home, and his parents immediately notified the police. The boy returned to guide a policeman, PC Frank Brown, to the spot, where the naked body of a man was found. Papers near the body identified him as 26 year old John Richardson. He had been a student at Cambridge, served in the Navy during the War, then returned to Cambridge.

He had changed to the Roman Catholic faith, and become extremely devout, even going to Ireland with the intention of taking Holy Orders, but returned to a business career in England. He told his family that he was going on a walking holiday, but he apparently found his way into the Caves where he fasted naked in darkness, presumably while meditating. Near the body was a rosary, and a rucksack containing his clothes. At the bottom of the rucksack, under everything else, was a torch. Dr F E Camps, pathologist, said that death was due to starvation and exposure. "The man had gone without food for about a week, and apparently collapse had come without warning. There was no suggestion of foul play. Summing up at the inquest, the North West Kent Coroner, Mr S O Matthews said "His father has given us a good insight into his past history, and there is nothing whatever to show us that he deliberately ended his life, but on the other hand such a position did not come about by accident or adventure".

They could only surmise that he had gone there for some purpose connected with religious devotions, but unfortunately had suddenly collapsed and died. "He did not realise his fast had taken him so far" said the Coroner, recording a verdict of Death from Exposure. Although the verdict was Death from Exposure, there was always a mystery of why a grown man, in good health, should suddenly expire. Mr Gardner, the wartime owner, told me that he had been called in to see the body, and in his opinion he looked terrified. There isn't a verdict in English law of "frightened to death", so perhaps the Coroner just got as close as he could...

A place the *Most Haunted* team reported as where someone died fits in with the location Mr Gardner told us. He wouldn't take us to the exact spot (we were, after all, only schoolboys) but as he was talking to us, and he just waved down a passage and said that the body was found "down there".

The Girl in the Caves Hospital

Although she looks quite innocent in the light, I have had a few children (and adults!) on tours who thought she looked frightening. The *Most Haunted* investigators got quite "spooked" by her during one of their vigils, during which they seemed to have several missiles thrown at them. Poltergeist activity is often said to be connected with young children...

Although she is only a dressed-up manikin (or should that be girlikin?), there *was* a death of a little girl there during the War. As Mr Gardner explained the story to us, it involved one of a group of children who were playing in the woods above the Caves. They had found a pit in the sand created when a tree had blown over, and were digging their own "cavelet" in the side when the hole collapsed, burying the little girl. Her friends raised the alarm and started to dig her out.

They were quickly joined by other people who had been standing around outside the Caves, and she was rushed down to the Caves hospital, where the Red Cross Nurses did what they could, but were unable to save her. It's very difficult to state with certainty exactly when somebody dies, so all we can say is that she died somewhere between the woods and the hospital, but the story has always been that she "died in the Caves hospital", which was where the *Most Haunted* team sensed a presence.

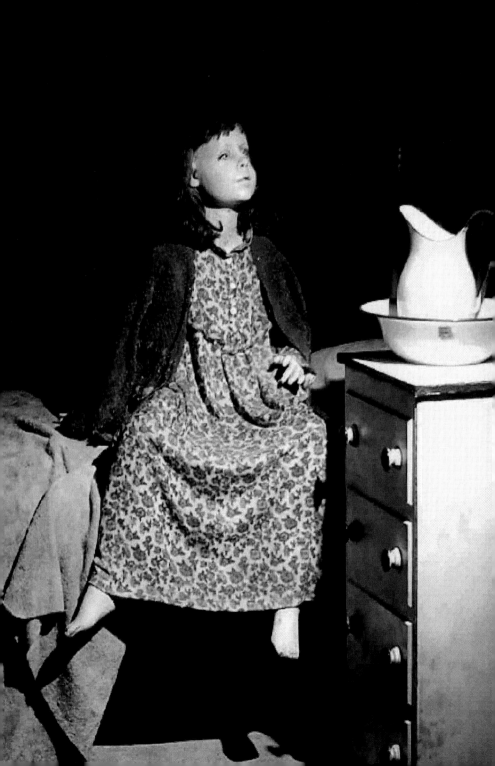

Labyrinthe Club. Noises in the dark...

At times, there are some parts of the Caves where you can hear bloodcurdling shouts and screams and, if you know where to look, you may glimpse a troll, Queen Boudicca or a Warrior Elf. Not as magic as it seems, actually. Part of the Caves are walled off and used by a Dungeons'n'Dragons Live Role Play group called the *Labyrinthe Club* (strictly Members Only!). The club members have built castle walls and dungeons, and run (or tip toe) around by the light of an occasional Glo-stick or candle.. The walls are there to keep them apart from the tours. After all, if a gang of Warrior Elves met up with a tour party, it might put them right off their feud... On days they are playing, you could find yourself sharing the Caves car park with Vlad the Impaler, a Viking Princess or a carload of hobgoblins ... but who's going to believe you when you tell them?

Scream Tours

There is a general human desire for excitement, and most people want to be frightened – at least a little bit. I had a beautiful example of this late in 2008. A birthday party had just gone in, when a dad and little boy turned up late, and I took them in to catch up with the rest of their friends. I'd only just got to the entrance hall when I got a radio call that someone else had just turned up, and would I take them too. Since we were still in the lit entrance, I asked the boy and his dad to wait while I popped back to collect the newcomer. It turned out to be a little girl by herself - mum brought her but didn't want to go down, so I took custody of the child for the few seconds it took to bring her down to the other two.

Children are not allowed lanterns, so although I had a torch, only the dad had a lantern, and the little girl was not impressed by the darkness.

The doorkeeper of the Labyrinthe Club is always ready to welcome new members!

In order not to let anyone down, I lent the little girl one of my spare torches to reassure her, but it was not very successful. There was a stream of "I don't like the dark!", "I want to go home" and "I want my Mummy!", but I guessed that she would cheer up as soon as we met up with the main party, whom I knew were not far in. Then we rounded a corner, and could see them just ahead. I was looking for the other Guide to warn him of the nervous little girl I was bringing him, when suddenly there's a screech beside me. She had turned the torch up to give her a scary face, and with a yell she announced "The Queen of Darkness is here!" Less than ten seconds separated "I want my mummy" to the arrival of "The Queen of Darkness". All she needed was an audience!

Another example is the little boy at the end of a Birthday party tour, who came up to the Guide and said "I've never been so frightened in my life – thank you!"

Over the years the guides have helped this desire to be frightened, told ghost stories and occasionally demonstrated their ingenuity by constructing devices to intrigue or startle visitors. The earliest record I have found is in a cinema newsreel from 1931, which shows a party of visitors being shown a fissure "from where smoke or steam is issuing". There is no such place now, so perhaps it was just an early disco smoke machine!

Special "themed" tours planned to scare the daylights out of visitors were run for many years. In the late 1950's we schoolboys occasionally helped out with the frightening process. My favourite was one section of the route where the tour put out their lights and felt their way along by following a rope, suspended like a handrail. A few strings suspended from the ceiling so they just brushed the visitors' hair was very effective, as was digging a hole and putting a sponge rubber cushion there – treading on something squishy when you couldn't see what it was puts the pulse rate up a bit.

Then one of us used to sit waiting a bit further along, with a container of cold water. We would hold our hands in the water until the last minute, then gently rest them on the guide rope. The unsuspecting visitor would suddenly come across a cold and clammy hand. The natural reaction is to take your hand away, then go back and feel for the person standing there. But we, of course, had been sitting down so there was nothing to find. And by the time they came to feel for the hand again, we were long gone, with any slight noise we made covered by the explanations (and occasional screams!) of the one who touched us, trying to get sympathy and explain why they stopped so suddenly.

Another favourite, when the visitors were walking by the light of a candle, was simply to walk out of the darkness some way in front of them, cross over and "disappear" down a side passage. We were dressed in grey, and wore plimsoles (these were the days before trainers) so we made little noise. We would know where we were going, and anyway could see quite well by the light of their candle, which also served to dazzle them. A variation was to walk towards them and blow out their candle in passing. Noisemakers, cackles, groans and shrieks were also used, in moderation. Clanking chains were effective, but difficult to keep quiet when not required.

These tours went on up to the late 1990's, when falling numbers made them no longer economical, since they were very labour-intensive. I suppose that with the increasing sophistication of theme park rides and horror films, people are getting their thrills elsewhere. A pity really, because some of the things devised for the later tours were absolutely fiendish, but I won't go into details – we might want to do them again, and we wouldn't want to spoil the surprises, would we?

The Guides' Stories...

There are usually two regular Guides, with others called in as needed for busy periods like school holidays or special booked tours. So there's a collection of Guides who work at the Caves occasionally and I asked them for their contributions. They had their own stories of odd occurrences. Many are unexplained noises. Noise travels considerable distances, and the sound of the drum used to demonstrate the echo can be heard over half a mile away. Some parties are quite high spirited, and the sound of laughter or even a giggle can travel a long way and get very distorted. It's only when you know that you are alone in the Caves that the hairs on the back of your neck stand up... That must be water dripping somewhere, mustn't it?

As Manager of the Caves, Terry Hunt spends most of his time in the office, and often talks to people coming out after a tour. He tells the following stories ... "One lady, who had just been round with her husband and little daughter, told me that at one point on the tour she suddenly felt her little daughter take her hand. Feeling sorry that she must be feeling a little frightened, she gave her hand a little squeeze, and got an answering squeeze. Shortly afterwards, she felt her hand released. She was at the back of the tour, and didn't have a lantern, so she couldn't see very well. Feeling a little concerned about her daughter, she pushed through the tour looking for her. She soon found her, near the front of the tour holding her Daddy's hand. Daddy assured Mummy that their little girl had been safe with him all the time. There had been no other children on that tour, which left the lady more than a little puzzled. So if you're holding a little hand in the dark, just check to see that it's who you think it is, will you? Everyone worries about losing people from a tour party, but we are a bit wary about gaining people, too!"

"Another lady, very excited, told me that she had seen a ghost while she was on her tour as they were going by the Cavaliers

Entrance. As she gushed her story, I realised what had happened. At that spot, Guides often have a location problem. It's on a corner, and with big tours Guides often ask the people at the front of the tour to move on ahead to the next corner to allow the Guide to show the passageway to the remainder of the party. This puts them at the wrong end of the group, so they have a choice: either push through to the front or go around another way. Luckily there is another way, and they usually put out their light and nip round a couple of corners to rejoin the tour at the front. Most people realise what has happened when their guide suddenly reappears at the front of the party, and off they go again. However, on this occasion she had obviously been towards the middle of the group, and not seen the guide leave the tail of the tour nor seen him reappear at the front. She had just seen a shadowy figure pass across the end of a side passage. No matter how much I tried to explain that she had probably just seen the guide on their way to the front of the tour, she was convinced that I was just covering up the truth so as not to scare the other people present. Thus are ghost stories started!"

Brian Williamson, the compiler of this book, has the distinction of having the longest connection with the Caves, having visited and worked in the Caves as a schoolboy and then joining as a Guide when he retired in 2003. He remembers some schoolboy antics: "It's possible that I started one ghost story. I brought in a couple of small round cycle reflectors, and placed them in a piece of chalk near to the Haunted Pool. The guide used to shine the beam of his torch on the wall of the pool as soon as he came out of Snowy Way, the little link tunnel from the Druids. But this time he illuminated a small creature with bright red eyes ... So if you hear of a small ghost with bright red eyes, it was all my fault, really. This is close to a place where I and a friend thought we had seen something we couldn't explain – an apparent hooded figure. We played about with various

37

positions for our candles, and finally concluded that one of our friends had moved a candle to a place where its light was shaped by a series of walls and corners to leave the "figure" we saw. We had regretfully to forget our ghost story!

On one occasion, in 2007, when talking to a party at the Haunted Pool, there was the sound of a door being slammed. Everyone turned towards me, waiting for me to explain, and I said that there must be people working in the Caves. When I got out, I checked with the office, who assured me that there were no builders or anybody else in the caves, and the Labyrinthe club were not in either. There are actually very few doors in the Caves now, all the wartime ones having rotted or rusted away. Those that remain are kept locked, and the office have the keys. I have never explained that noise!"

Desmond Tyler tells of encounters with vanishing strangers... "I was taking a tour round a few years ago, and had just finished explaining something which had all the party looking to their front, and as I turned round to lead on to the next item I found myself face to face with a stranger - absolutely close up, almost touching. I was sure that there had been no-one there before I started. As a guide you get into the habit of knowing where your party are, and obviously you don't stand right in front of anybody if you can help it. I was so startled that I took a step back, and turned to see if anybody in the party had noticed, but they were all still looking at the previous exhibit.

I turned back to ask the stranger where he had come from - but he wasn't there any more. It gave me quite a turn, I can tell you! When I finished the tour I mentioned the occurrence to other guides, expecting them to laugh at me, but several of them went quiet and confessed that something similar had happened to them. One part-time guide apparently refused to come back for months..." When the Guides discussed it amongst themselves, it became evident that it was always at

38

the same place... He also tells of an occasion when he spotted someone walk round a corner and turn into the Map Room near the entrance. Not wishing to lose a member of his tour, he chased after them, only to find when he got there that the room was empty and there was no way out.

Nick Winter was nearly pushed over in front of a tour he was taking round one evening... "The guides occasionally challenge each other to find their way round the tour totally in the dark. Difficult, but not impossible after a few years experience. Several of us when attempting this challenge found ourselves "assisted" when we hesitated for a moment by a shove in the right direction. Lady guides who attempted the challenge received a gentle push, but men could get quite a shove. This usually only happens in the dark, but it happened to me once in front of an entire tour party. I was taking a party round on a late evening tour and hesitated, not sure which route would interest the visitors more, when I suddenly received such a shove that I nearly fell over. I thought that somebody from my party had pushed me, but there was nobody near enough to have done so. Several of the party were looking at me, wondering what made me stagger and nearly fall, but nobody had seen the cause."

Chris Perry was one of the Guides taking part in the Challenge in 1985. As Chief Guide, he had the job of opening the Caves at the start of each day. As he explains, "Because of possible vandalism the entrances to the Caves are closed at night by close fitting steel doors, which have to be unlocked. The main doors are fastened by a padlock, and to make them more secure, the padlock is on the inside of the door. There is a small hole just big enough to put your hand through, and you have to fiddle with the keys by touch. One morning I put my hand through the hole in the door - and felt another, cold, hand. Luckily I was wearing brown trousers. I rushed back to the Guides office and got someone else to come down with me. They had no trouble at all with the door, and it soon became obvious that I had been set up - one of the other Guides had come in especially early through another entrance, and had been waiting for me. But I always felt a tingle of anticipation whenever I opened the door after that!"

Dan McLean, a one-time regular Guide, spent a lot of time underground, both leading tours and doing chores about the place. Although unperturbed by the majority of the miles of passageways, there was one particular doorway that used to send shivers up his spine if he had to go past it. And he definitely didn't like to go through it...

Barbara Viahakis, a lady Guide, has no time to spare for talk of ghosts and the like, and refuses to admit the possibility that such things exist. However, even she will admit to experiencing something she can't explain. "I was taking a tour around the end of 2007 when it happened by the Cavaliers' Passage. I was explaining the details to a group of approximately 10 adults when suddenly the torch I as holding was 'yanked back'. I turned around, thinking that maybe there was a child behind me playing a prank. But, no, there were only adults in the group and there was no one behind me at all. That's the only unexplainable occurrence I have experienced – at least, so far!"

Paul Andrews, the most experienced of the Guides, tells of a tour which included a small boy. At one place, he suddenly turned to his mother and asked "Mummy, who is that funny lady standing over there?" Seems a reasonable question, except that nobody else could see anybody there at all.

He also remembers "On one occasion a young lady in a school party asked me whether I could also see a green glow at the end of a passage, or was she seeing things that weren't there? (or worse, seeing things that were there but only she could see!). I was able to reassure her that she was seeing a real phenomenon, not a ghostly one. She was very brave to bring it to my attention, and it is to the credit of her school that they develop such confident pupils – most adults simply pretend that they haven't seen anything! There usually isn't anything to see at that place, anyway. What happens is that there is a disused wartime fan shaft there, and although there are walls to prevent entry both at the top and bottom of the shaft, small holes have been left to allow air to circulate. At certain times, sunlight shines down the shaft, and reflects round several corners, appearing as a slight glow from some places. At some seasons, since there is overhanging vegetation at the top of the shaft, the light appears green. A very simple and natural series of events. But if you are not expecting it, it can make the hair on the back of your neck stand up!"

Chrissy Selby, an attractive lady guide, remembers a meeting with what must have been a male ghost. "I was walking through the Caves by myself, doing what we call a litter trip - going round the tour route with a bag picking up discarded sweet wrappers and so on. Since we ask all visitors not to eat and drink in the Caves, there shouldn't be any, but some seem to happen anyway. As usual, I was using a collector to save bending down too much, but came upon a toffee paper firmly trodden down, and bent down to pick it up. It was mid-summer, and I was wearing a mini-skirt. Suddenly a breeze fluttered my skirt, and I distinctly heard a wolf whistle. Most disconcerting, since I knew I was alone in the Caves and there are no sudden breezes down there, but I decided to take it as a compliment. Mind you, I tend to wear trousers in the Caves now!"

Rod LeGear, the most scientific and level-headed of the guides, simply doesn't believe in ghosts and says nothing has ever happened to him! However, a visitor mentioned at the end of a tour that he had experienced a cold chill at one point, and was convinced that he had experienced a contact from the Spirit World. Having worked out where this had taken place, Rod was able to explain that there was often a slight temperature gradient around there, which some sensitive people could detect. However, the man was unconvinced, and went off sure he had "touched the other side"!

Once when he was leaving a small party in the dark at the Druid's Altar he invited them to imagine a party of Druid priests tramping up the passageway toward them, and suggested that if they listened carefully, they might even hear them chanting as they came. Later on the tour a lady assured him that she had heard the chanting, and congratulated him on the excellent sound effects. He hadn't got the heart to explain that there are no sound effects there...

Jeffry Hooton had his introduction to the mysteries of the Caves soon after joining. He told me "As a new tour guide I was sceptical of the ghostly stories linked to the Caves, and wondered whether I would ever see a ghost or even an unexplained shadow? My first few weeks were exciting. I met many interesting people, learned a little of the Caves' history, and settled into a comfortable routine.

It was an early morning tour just after my first cup of tea (yes, I am an American, but this is England, so I drink tea like the locals!) My first tour group of the day was a group of six French College students who were excited about the Caves, and I was in the sort of mood to give them a scary tour in the darkness. Little did I realise it would be me who would experience the cold terror, chilling fear and confusion of the Caves. The tour started out normally, with the group asking the typical tourist questions and giggling along the way at a few of my ghostly comments.

As we were going through the Druids I noticed that I felt colder than normal. Knowing that there were no draughts in the Caves, I thought that perhaps I was just not dressed warmly enough and dismissed the chill. As the tour progressed, my chill became ever present. Normally I am quite comfortable in the Caves, but this particular morning I was ice cold. Soon I would discover why. I begun to notice a tugging on my sweater. It was as if a small child was holding on to my sweater so as to avoid being lost. I had no small children on the tour and just assumed someone's hand was bumping me in the dark. Soon I couldn't ignore the tugging any more as it persisted past the next stopping point, which happened to be the Druid Altar, and became more powerful and purposeful. I knew something was happening, but what I couldn't say. I continued the tour as normally as I could and set aside my fear as I talked to my group about the Haunted Pool.

Suddenly the tugging stopped. I was relieved, but only momentarily. As I looked at my group I realised that a new face had appeared. Along with the group of six college students was a seventh person. A small child of 7 or 8 was visible at the back of the group. He was wearing a brown leather Derby cap, a blazer and short brown pants. His shoes were black with tattered laces. This was not someone who began the tour with me. I was just about to ask if he had become lost when I realised something peculiar about him. His face was clear to see, but was slightly transparent, and I could also see the wall behind him. He was emotionless, like an empty shell of a person whose soul had been taken from him. I could barely talk as I tried to continue my tour. I was curious, but afraid. I decided that my best course of action would be to approach the boy. I walked over to him, and as I did so he simply drifted into the darkness of the Caves from which he had come. I have never heard of any sightings like this in the Caves before, nor have I ever seen the child again.

Could it have been a lost soul trapped in the Caves years ago, or just my imagination catching up with me? I may never know."

(Editor: A very curious story. What Jeff didn't know was that there was a death of a little a boy sheltering in the Caves during the War. He was with his mother, and went playing in the woods above the Caves with several of his friends when he gashed his leg on an old log. He was brought into the Caves for First Aid, and the Red Cross Nurses patched up the wound, but decided it was too serious for them to deal with, and sent him to hospital. Unfortunately, he died about two weeks later in hospital from an infection, probably tetanus. These were the days before antibiotics, and tetanus claimed many victims. We've never before counted his death as being connected with the Caves, and it is odd that the first sighting should be to an American. However, we'll all keep a special watch out on the children on our tours in future!)

Jason Desporte, a full-time guide, had this tale to tell:
"One morning, shortly after being hired at the caves, by about 2 months, I arrived at work quite early. I was the first person there. After lighting all the lanterns, I decided to do a quick walk through the Caves and make sure all was fine and none of lights were out. As I made my way through the Druid's near the Roman well I heard a noise behind me. I stopped, turned around and looked but nothing was there, just then I heard a giggle like that of a little girl behind me, I quickly turned, shined my torch but again there was nothing. Just as I was about to walk off I distinctively heard the giggling and laughing of what sounded like a little girl that was running about. As I turned and looked carefully again I saw nothing. At this point I figured that someone had arrived and was playing a joke on me. So I finished my walk through and went back up top. When I arrived to the office to my surprise there was no one there and the building was still locked. I said nothing about the incident because it started to get busy quite early and I just figured I was hearing things. That was until about a week later while talking in the office with other guides and the owner Jim. Somehow my little incident came

44

into conversation and that's when Jim said, I must talking about the little girl that during the War had been digging a large hole above the Caves entrance with her brother. However it collapsed in on them, killing her but not her brother. And that because she used to play in the Caves with the other children it is believed that she still plays in there now. I was shocked to hear this because the one thing about this story is, I had never been told about the incident before and I never heard it told by any other guides because it is not a story told on the cave tours. One thing though, I hope she's having fun."

Stefan Zambinski had an interesting introduction to the Caves. "Before I worked as a tour guide I also worked in the café situated at the entrance to the cave system. I built up friendships with the guides that worked there at that time and spent many lunch breaks working out crosswords in the small office used by the tour guides. One day I decided to have a look inside the Caves after working in the café for some time but not going into the Caves themselves. I walked through the concrete tunnel that leads into the cave system, on my own for the first time, and went on through the entrance hall. I noticed that there was a light coming from the passage ahead of me, past where the entrance hall lights ended. I assumed that one of the Guides must be working down there. Feeling in need of a little company, I decided to go that way and see what they were up to. The light was moving ahead of me, as though someone was carrying a lantern, so I hurried up to catch them – or at least see who it was. Just round the corner was the Hospital exhibit, with light streaming out of the door. I called out, but got no reply, so I lifted the rope across the entrance and went in. Apart from the dummy exhibits, there was no one there. Then I realised that the only footsteps I could hear were mine, and there had been no sound apart from me breathing.

I retraced my steps out to the lit entrance (a bit faster than I had come in!) and went back up to the office, which suddenly seemed a very warm and friendly place! The other Guides there, noticing that I was panting, asked me if I was all right, and I told them my story. They confirmed that nobody had gone in before me, and all the Guides had been in the office all the time. They decided that it was probably just that the little girl in the hospital was feeling lonely and encouraged me to visit her! I felt that I had been welcomed to the Caves, and this settled my ambition to apply for a job as an occasional Guide. I'm now fully trained and lead tours through the Caves. But I've still got a soft spot for the little girl who invited me in that first time, and one time I am sure that she winked at me!"

The Frightened Man

There is one presence that several of the Guides think they have seen. Some of the guides have parts of the Caves where they feel uncomfortable - nothing specific, just a vague unease - and when we compared notes, we found that most of us chose the same areas. After some prompting, several of the guides admitted to seeing the figure of a frightened man at one point.

Listening to all the accounts, Paul Andrews, Caves Guide and our resident artist, came up with a picture which we all agreed was similar to what we had seen.

If you see him, let your Guide know – but please do it quietly without alarming the rest of the tour. He's never been known to hurt anybody, and we seem to frighten him as much as he can startle us!

This character, known as the **Necromancer,** (a kind of senior wizard) was frequently seen in the Caves, but after an argument with the owner, has not been seen for about twenty years. However, we feel that he is not far away, so keep an eye out for him...

Rats, Bats and Spiders

One question we Guides are often asked is "Are there any rats down here?", and the answer is NO. There are several theories advanced to explain this, and readers are invited to review them and choose for themselves.

1. Since Visitors are discouraged from bringing food on tours, there are no crumbs or wrappers, so no insects, therefore no food for rats, either.
2. The partnership of Chalky, the Caves Cat, and Gordon

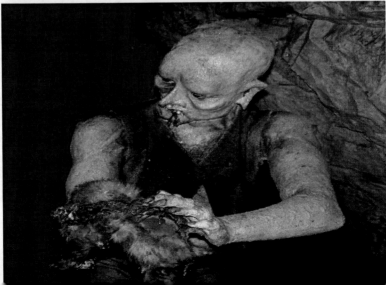

the Gremlin, who lives in the Caves near the entrance. Between them they catch and eat any rats who dare to try to enter.

3. Or is it perhaps because the Dragons have eaten them all?

But if all that fails, the Caves management have a contract with a Herr P Piper of Hamlein in Germany. He is skilled in dealing with rats, and would take away any who did manage to enter. However, he has been troubled by non-payers before, so we would have to be very certain to pay him his due if ever we used his services, or the next birthday Party tour might have problems. As a final back-up, a leading figure in the City of London, Mr R Whittington, and his faithful assistant would be asked to help.

Bats

Although bats have occasionally been seen in the Caves - twice in the past 50 years, to my knowledge - these are only tourists and soon depart, as they find the temperature too warm for them. Outside is a different story.

One of the Cave's Bat friends

If you stand in the car park and look around, there is a good chance that you will spot a couple of bats that are often seen hanging around. Please don't frighten them away, as they wake up in the evenings and do a good job catching insects after we've all gone home.

Spiders
There are none in the Caves. There may be a few around the entrance, but only as far as the daylight reaches.

Be good in the car park, you never know who may be watching you!

Getting lost

This is a thing many people are anxious about, but you would have to work really hard to get lost. Teachers are the most concerned, and have been known to completely spoil the kids' enjoyment of a visit by over-protection. Young children have a natural caution, and although they will make a lot of noise about their independence, they somehow never get outside the pool of light from the lanterns carried on the tour.

Teenagers are occasionally a problem. A few show off by dodging round a chalk pillar and reappearing round a corner, but you can't do that everywhere. Some parts of the Caves have walls put up during the War to direct the airflow from the fans, so if you dodge round a corner you can find your way blocked by a wall. If you are sensible, you turn back and rejoin the tour, and nobody is any the wiser. If you rush on, you may meet another wall, then another... At that point they usually call out, try to retrace their steps (but the Caves can look very different going back!) Then, if they are lucky, they meet the Guide coming to meet them. The Rule is to stay where you are and wait. There will probably be another tour round in a day or two.

Some clever people plan for getting lost. One visitor proudly announced that he had cracked the problem - he was going to take a piece of chalk with him and draw arrows on the wall as he went round. Although this might have worked in a coal mine, it isn't a very good idea in a chalk mine!

Other regular suggestions are to leave a trail of breadcrumbs or to unwind a ball of string as you go. One practical problem is the size of the ball of string or the loaf necessary to leave a trail about a mile long, but don't forget to keep looking behind you to see what has discovered your trail and is now busy following after *you*...

Ghosts you can eat!

Birthday Parties can have a special tour, visiting low tunnels and the Dr Who Caves, with a special test for the brave at the Druid's Altar, then a party meal in the Caves Cafe. As an extra, the Caves can arrange for a special cake to be baked and decorated just for the occasion. Whatever you can imagine, it can be done, and we have had dragons guarding piles of gold, skulls, cauldrons full of horrible things - or it could be a football or a Fairy Palace. You choose!

Just call the Caves Cafe and they can book your party meal and put you in touch with our award-winning artistic baker, Debbie Fairweather, or email: cakesofart@btconnect.com, or visit www.cakesofart.co.uk

Photo Ghosts

There are two photographic oddities which visitors often bring to our attention - *orbs* and *mist*. In both cases, the photographer always insists that there was nothing there when the picture was taken, but found something unexpected when they looked at the pictures later.

Orbs are unexpected white or pale circular spots which can be seen on some pictures. Every picture containing orbs that I have ever seen simply showed some out of focus dust particles. You never used to get them, but you do nowadays. Believers try to convince me that this is due to a recent increase in the number of spirits trying to make contact with the living. I try to convince them that it is simply due to the reduction in size of modern cameras, which puts the built-in flash much closer to the lens, and much more liable to bounce light back from innocent dust particles.

Mist is another event entirely. The temperature in the Caves is about 10 degrees Centigrade, just about cold enough for breath to form misty clouds. At certain temperatures it is quite possible for the cloud of breath to form very tiny droplets, which act as a reflector. You can't see them when the light is coming from an angle, but again, the flash near the lens shows them up well. The simple way to avoid creating mist is to hold your breath when taking a picture - but do remember to start again, or you may be included in the next edition of this book!

This is not so much a problem nowadays, since we have had to restrict visitors from taking photographs in the dark. Modern cameras have very powerful flashes, and we were getting complaints from other visitors on tours who were getting dazzled by the flashes. So no more flash photography in the dark!

Victorian Illusions

You may think that we are fascinated by ghosts today, but this is nothing like the interest a century ago. In the days before TV, when even photography and radio were still inventors playthings, everybody had to entertain themselves. All young people were expected to learn to play an instrument or sing, and evenings would be spent in the Drawing Room round the piano with each family member taking it in turns to perform.

Naturally, outside entertainment was very welcome, and Music Halls were very popular. In country areas touring performers would be offered space in local barns or halls, but a purpose-built theatre was favourite, since it allowed for scenery, and special effects. Lighting would be dim – probably only gas lights, with an occasional special light obtained by a gas flame on a piece of lime, which glowed brightly when heated. We still talk of "being in the limelight". The atmosphere would be smoky, from all the gas or oil lamps. The "magic lantern" was still so new that people would pay to go and see one in use, and a still picture projected on a wall was a novelty. So, audiences were ready to believe in new wonders, and yearned for Ghosts. This was an age of frequent new technical developments and discoveries, such as the wireless (radio), medical advances, (and stories like Dracula and Frankenstein!) telegraphy (the telephone), the first flying machines, photography, electricity (which allowed for brighter lights), horseless carriages (the motor car) and railways.

With all these developments, surely it wouldn't take long before someone found out how to contact the dead? Whenever you have an unfulfilled desire like that, somebody will step forward to satisfy it for you – at a price. Music Halls created ghosts to entertain their audiences. A French Conjurer, Robin, created an illusion big enough for the theatre. In the picture, the man in black is putting his arm right through the "Ghost"! Real Ghosts are difficult to organise to appear on stage as required, of course, but if you can't deliver the real thing, then a bit of trickery or illusion will have to do.

This illusion uses a plain sheet of glass at an angle. The audience could see through it, and didn't realise it was there, but it reflected whatever was in the right place below it, when the lighting was right, which was when the man below the stage put his light on.

You can get the same effect nowadays whenever you look out of a window, and can see the inside of the room reflected at the same time as the outside. Like all tricks, it seems obvious when you know how it is done, but to the Victorians it seemed like magic! The same principle is in regular use today. Have you ever wondered how the TV newsreader manages to memorise all the news each night?

Well, they don't. They are looking at an angled sheet of glass, which reflects a small TV screen showing the words they have to say, called an Autocue. The TV camera "looks" straight through the glass to the newsreader. Jet pilots have a similar device allowing them to look straight ahead, and see their gun sight and important instruments apparently in the sky ahead of them. All thanks to Victorian inventors making ghosts for their audiences!

A simple version of this was developed for travelling showmen which projected a picture onto a column of smoke. You may have heard an expression "it's all smoke and mirrors" meaning that something is an illusion, with no basis in reality. As you can see, this *really* is "all smoke and mirrors!"

Few people today would be fooled for a moment by these tricks, but there is still a desire in most people to believe in ghosts. People come to the Caves *wanting* to see something unexplained, so it's not surprising that some people do. There are no fake ghosts in the Caves, so any you see are all in your mind – or perhaps they are real? But before you start to dismiss our ancestors as a load of cranks, just think for a moment. Have you never kissed under the mistletoe, thrown a coin into a well for good luck, or read your horoscope in a newspaper? Most people still do – and these beliefs go back to Celtic times! So perhaps you aren't as disbelieving as you thought you were...

"Lost Tunnels"

All the Guides hear tales of "secret" or "lost" passages, connecting the Caves with every large old building in the neighbourhood, or even The Tower of London or Woolwich Arsenal. We Guides are a very cynical lot, and have heard most of the possible stories before. I once had a very intense lady telling me about the tunnel from Coopers School, about a mile away, and certainly their original building is several hundred years old. I pointed out the usual answer, that during the War they were so desperate for room for extra bunks that every possible wall was tested for additional Caves and any entrance would have been found. Any entrance that escaped their attentions would surely have been found by the hundreds of children playing "hide and seek" during the War years. No, she said triumphantly, the entrance was under the haunted pool! Even the escaper's at Colditz never thought of that one!

Another regular tale involves the building now used by Chislehurst Golf Club, close by the Caves on Chislehurst Common. Camden Place was a palace used by Emperor Napoleon III and his Empress Eugene. They are reputed to have used part of the Caves for storage, so just perhaps there is and we just haven't found it yet!

Author's Note: You may have noticed that I have been careful not to be specific about the location of some events. This is deliberate, since I don't want would-be mediums interrupting tours when they recognise a location and claiming to "feel the spirit world". If they are that good, they will know without being told, won't they?

Index

If you wish to correct an error or contribute to future editions of this book, please go to <u>www.nullpublishing.co.uk</u> and use the feedback page. Thank you!

Other books about Chislehurst Caves.

A Child's Wartime Memories. Jill Cheeseman

The memories of a child shelterer in the Caves.

Chislehurst Caves. A short History by Dr Eric Inman.

Both available from the Gift shop in the Caves, together with a selection of postcards and souvenirs.

Titles in course of preparation from Null Publishing:

A Place of Safety
A collection of memories from people who shelterered in Chislehurst Caves during the Second World War

The People's Music
The story of the music scene in the Caves, particularly skiffle, folk, jazz and rock'n'roll in the postwar years.

If you have any memories, stories or photographs in or about the Caves, or would like to arrange a talk for your club, please contact us!

Visit www.nullpublishing.co.uk or email: nullpublishing@tiscali.co.uk

How to get to Chislehurst Caves

By Rail. Chislehurst Station is on the Charing Cross to Orpington line. The next nearest railway station is **Bickley** (Victoria to Orpington or Sevenoaks line), then 162 or 269 bus to Chislehurst Station.

By Bus. Buses 162 *(Beckenham, Bromley, Bickley, Chislehurst, Eltham, about every 20 mins)* or 269 *(Bromley North, Bickley, Chislehurst, Sidcup, Bexleyheath), about every 10 - 15 mins)* both stop near Chislehurst railway station.

From Chislehurst Railway Station. The Caves are just around the corner. From the station, go down the hill to the left, turn right past the Bickley Arms in to Old Hill, turn right into Caveside Close and follow the signs.

By Car. A222 from Bromley or Sidcup to Chislehurst Station. Although the postcode is BR7 5NB, Sat-Nav users should enter **BR7 5NL** to avoid getting led astray! There are two large, free, car parks.

The Caves are generally open Wednesdays to Sundays, and additionally on Mondays and Tuesdays during local school holidays. General guided tours hourly from 10am to 4pm, with special school, club, birthday party or evening tours by arrangement. For the latest details call 020 8467 3264 or see the Caves websites at **www.chislehurstcaves.co.uk** or **www.chislehurst-caves.co.uk** There are lots of websites which mention the Caves, some of which are many years out of date. Please take care to check the right website!

At the start of this book you were asked whether or not you believed in Ghosts. If, after reading this, you still aren't sure, you should pay us a visit. It may help you to make up your mind!